Well! I Sure Didn't Know That

By

Morey Lokken

authorHOUSE™

1663 Liberty Drive, Suite 200
Bloomington, Indiana 47403
(800) 839-8640
www.AuthorHouse.com

First published by AuthorHouse 12/14/04

ISBN: 1-4208-0351-4 (e)
ISBN: 1-4208-0350-6 (sc)

Library of Congress Control Number: 2004097751

Printed in the United States of America
Bloomington, Indiana

This book is printed on acid-free paper.

Acknowledgements

I appreciate the love and support of those who inspired me. These individuals include: Dick Middlestead, Carol Hesse, Luke Wood, Bob Richardson, Trish Jacobs, Bud Keys, Sandy Bennett, Beverly Ferreira, my daughter Jeanette Nelson, my son-in-law Scott Nelson, and my grandchildren Caleb, Eric, and Kendra.

I am also indebted to my grandfather, Charlie Nelson, who planted the seeds for my love of God's word. Every morning and evening, he would gather the family and share God's word.

This book is being given with love and care.

To:

_____

From:

_____

So That's Where That May Have Come From

The clichés and phrases contained in this book are meant to be food for thought and to open up discussions.

How many Christians and non-Christians use these words daily and do not know where they may have originated.

This book is meant to be purchased and left in any professional or nonprofessional office where someone waiting may have a minute to relax and read.

It can be purchased from your local Bible bookstore or by ordering direct from the publisher.

Table of Contents

x

To Cover A Multitude Of Sins

Say! We have to cover that multitude of sins someway. Maybe we can do it with paint.

And above all things have fervent charity among yourselves: for charity shall cover the multitude of sins.
KJB   I PETER 4:8

Let him know, that he which converteth the sinner from the error of his way, shall save a soul from death, and shall hide a multitude of sins.
KJB   JAMES 5:20

I am a hobbyist with wood and metal. I make mistakes and I'm always looking for ways to cover them so I'm the only one to know.

If we confess our sins, he is faithful and just to forgive us *our* sins, and to cleanse us from all unrighteousness.
KJB   I JOHN 1:9

By The Skin Of My Teeth

Let me tell you, I missed by the skin on my teeth.

My bone cleaveth to my skin and to my flesh, and I am escaped with the skin on my teeth.
KJB   JOB 19:20

Will you escape being sent to hell by the skin of your teeth?

Will you make a decision for Christ today so you can be assured of having eternal life with Christ?

A friend asked me, "Do I need works to be saved?" The answer is No, No, No. But you must believe that Christ is the son of God and have faith in him to save you from your sins.

It is a free gift. You cannot buy it by works. However, because Christ died for my sins, I *want* to show him my pleasure by doing his will.

The Bible says that Christ died on the cross for our sins. If you believe this and ask him into your heart, you will have eternal life.

To ask him into your heart, turn to page 101 through 104. Read and follow these steps.

A String Around My Finger

My mother used to say to me, "Shall I tie a string around your finger? Then will you remember?"

As parents and grandparents we must teach our children right from wrong. We must set examples as the Hebrews did in times long ago. What we show them today may look as if it's not sinking in. But as they become adults, they will recall the bits of string we tied around their fingers when they were children to help them remember.

And these words, which I command thee this day, shall be in thine heart:

And thou shalt teach them diligently unto thy children, and shalt talk of them when thou sittest in thine house, and when thou walkest by the way, and when thou liest down, and when thou risest up.

And thou shalt bind them for a sign upon thine hand, and they shall be as frontlets between thine eyes.

And thou shalt write them upon the posts of thy house, and on thy gates.

KJB   DEUTERONOMY 6:6-9

I Bit My Tongue

I had to bite my tongue to keep from speaking out.

He that is void of wisdom despiseth his neighbour: but a man of understanding holdeth his peace.

KJB   PROVERBS 11:12

When you're a part of a group and someone is unjustly being put down, be bold and say something good about that individual.

We argue with others to convince them of our truth. That never works. When we live our truths, change takes place in our neighbor's heart.

The Blind Leading The Blind

Talk about the blind leading the blind.

Let them alone: they be blind leaders of the blind. And if the blind lead the blind, both shall fall into the ditch.
KJB   MATTHEW 15:14

Jesus is teaching us about the spiritually blind. The question is who are the spiritually blind?

They are those who say they are teaching from the Bible. But when you ask them to show you where in the Bible, they cannot.

What can we do to help?

We can show them the truth through chapters and verses from the Bible and lead them to a Group Bible Study.

Thrown To The Lions

Have you ever heard the expression, "He or she is being thrown to the lions?"

Then the king commanded, and they brought Daniel, and cast *him* into the den of lions. *Now* the king spake and said unto Daniel, Thy God whom thou servest continually, he will deliver thee.
KJB   DANIEL 6:16

God did save Daniel and the king was so impressed that he issued a decree that stated, in every part of his kingdom, people must fear and worship the God of Daniel.

Please read DANIEL Chapter 6 for the complete story.

Jezebel

When you call a woman a jezebel, you're saying that she is a revengeful person, a murderess, and is someone who provokes others to evil.

Jezebel was married to the wicked King Ahad.

Please read I KINGS 21. This chapter will give you insight on how wicked Queen Jezebel lived her life.

God says we are not to judge others. When we call someone a jezebel, we are doing what God has asked us not to do.

Red Sky In The Morning

Red sky in the morning, sailor's warning.
Red sky at night, sailor's delight.

The Pharisees also with the Sadducees came, and tempting desired him that he would shew them a sign from heaven.

He answered and said unto them, When it is evening, ye say, *It will be* fair weather: for the sky is red.

And in the morning, *It will be* foul weather to-day: for the sky is red and lowering. O *ye* hypocrites, ye can discern the face of the sky; but can ye not *discern* the signs of the times?
KJB MATTHEW 16:1-3

The Star Of Jesus' Birth

When we say he or she is a star, we think of the movies. But where did the word star in the form of a person originate?

Now when Jesus was born in Bethlehem of Judaea in the days of Herod the king, behold, there came wise men from the east to Jerusalem,

Saying, Where is he that is born King of the Jews? for we have seen his star in the east, and are come to worship him.
KJB   MATTHEW 2:1-2

A Scapegoat

How often have you heard someone say, "This person is being used as a scapegoat?"

This comes from the Book of LEVITICUS in the Old Testament.

And he shall take of the congregation of the children of Israel two kids of the goats for a sin offering, and one ram for a burnt offering.

And Aaron shall offer his bullock of the sin offering, which *is* for himself, and make an atonement for himself, and for his house.

And he shall take the two goats, and present them before the LORD *at* the door of the tabernacle of the congregation.

And Aaron shall cast lots upon the two goats; one lot for the LORD, and the other lot for the scapegoat.

And Aaron shall bring the goat upon which the LORD'S lot fell, and offer him *for* a sin offering.

But the goat, on which the lot fell to be the scapegoat, shall be presented alive before the LORD, to make an atonement with him, *and* to let him go for a scapegoat into the wilderness.
KJB   LEVITICUS 16:5-10

A Thief Returns To His Crime

A thief often times returns to the scene of the crime. Or, an arsonist will stay and watch what he has set on fire.

As a dog returneth to his vomit, *so* a fool returneth to his folly.
KJB   PROVERBS 26:11

Doubting Thomas

He or she is like a doubting Thomas, which reminds me of the state of Missouri's motto: "Show Me."

But Thomas, one of the twelve, called Didymus, was not with them when Jesus came.

The other disciples therefore said unto him, We have seen the Lord. But he said unto them, Except I shall see in his hands the print of the nails, and put my finger into the print of the nails, and thrust my hand into his side, I will not believe.

After eight days again his disciples were within, and Thomas with them: *then* came Jesus, the doors being shut, and stood in the midst, and said, Peace *be* unto you,

Then saith he to Thomas, Reach hither thy finger, and behold my hands; and reach hither thy hand, and thrust *it* into my side: and be not faithless, but believing.

And Thomas answered and said unto him, My Lord and my God.

Jesus saith unto him, Thomas, because thou hast seen me, thou hast believed: blessed *are* they that have not seen, and *yet* have believed.
KJB   JOHN 20:24-29

Please read HEBREWS 11. This chapter is about faith. The people believed without always seeing. They are good examples for us.

Note: There is a time to doubt and a time to believe.

Deviled Ham

Could it be that the word deviled ham originated from the Book of MARK?

And they came over unto the other side of the sea, into the country of the Gadarenes.

And when he was come out of the ship, immediately there met him out of the tombs a man with an unclean spirit,

Who had *his* dwelling among the tombs; and no man could bind him, no, not with chains:

Because that he had been often bound with fetters and chains, and the chains had been plucked asunder by him, and the fetters broken in pieces: neither could any *man* tame him.

And always, night and day, he was in the mountains, and in the tombs, crying, and cutting himself with stones.

But when he saw Jesus afar off, he ran and worshipped him.

And cried with a loud voice, and said, What have I to do with thee, Jesus, *thou* Son of the most high God? I adjure thee by God, that thou torment me not.

For he said unto him, Come out of the man, *thou* unclean spirit.

And he asked him, What *is* thy name? And he answered, saying, My name *is* Legion: for we are many.

And he besought him much that he would not send them away out of the country.

Now there was there nigh unto the mountains a great herd of swine feeding.

And all the devils besought him, saying, Send us into the swine, that we many enter into them.

And forthwith Jesus gave them leave. And the unclean spirits went out, and entered into the swine: and the herd ran violently down a steep place into the sea, (they were about two thousand;) and were choked in the sea.

KJB MARK 5:1-13

Passing The Buck

Who was the first man to do what we commonly refer to as "Passing the Buck?"

And the LORD God called unto Adam, and said unto him, Where *art* thou?

And he said, I heard thy voice in the garden, and I was afraid, because I *was* naked; and I hid myself.

And he said, Who told thee that thou *wast* naked? Hast thou eaten of the tree, whereof I commanded thee that thou shouldest not eat?

And the man said, The woman whom thou gavest *to be* with me, she gave me the tree, and I did eat.

And the LORD God said unto the woman, What *is* this *that* thou hast done? And the woman said, The serpent beguiled me, and I did eat.

KJB GENESIS 3:9-13

More times than not when we pass the buck, we lose rather than gain. Be accountable for what you do.

Babbles On and On

How many times have we heard someone say, "He or she just babbles on and on?

And the whole earth was of one language, and of one speech.

And it came to pass, as they journeyed from the east, that they found a plain in the land of Shinar; and they dwelt there.

And they said one to another, Go to, let us make brick, and burn them throughly. And they had brick for stone, and slime had they for mortar.

And they said, Go to, let us build us a city and a tower, whose top *may reach* unto heaven; and let us make us a name, lest we be scattered abroad upon the face of the whole earth.

And the LORD came down to see the city and the tower, which the children of men builded.

And the LORD said, Behold, the people *is* one, and they have all one language; and this they begin to do: and now nothing will be restrained from them, which they have imagined to do.

Go to, let us go down, and there confound their language, that thy may not understand one another's speech.

So the LORD scattered them abroad from thence upon the face of all the earth: and they left off to build the city.

Therefore is the name of it call Babel; because the LORD did there confound the language of all the earth: and from thence did the LORD scatter them abroad upon the face of all the earth.

KJB   GENESIS 11:1-9

You Shall Know The Truth

And you shall know the truth and the truth shall set you free.

Several places of learning have this motto engraved on the entrances.

Many recognize this statement but take the meaning for something other than what it was meant to mean.

Jesus saith unto him, I am the way, the truth, and the life: no man cometh unto the Father, but by me.

KJB   JOHN 14:6

The only way we can have eternal life instead of eternal existence in hell is by accepting Jesus Christ as our personal savior.

And ye shall know the truth, and the truth shall make you free.

KJB   JOHN 8:32

A Good Samaritan

This person is really being a good Samaritan.

And Jesus answering said, A certain *man* went down from Jerusalem to Jericho, and fell among thieves, which stripped him of his raiment, and wounded *him*, and departed, leaving *him* half dead.

And by chance there came down a certain priest that way: and when he saw him, he passed by on the other side.

And likewise a Levite, when he was at the place, came and looked *on him*, and passed by on the other side.

But a certain Samaritan, as he journeyed, came where he was: and when he saw him, he had compassion *on him*,

And went to *him*, and bound up his wounds, pouring in oil and wine, and set him on his own beast, and brought him to an inn, and took care of him.

And on the morrow when he departed, he took out two pence, and gave *them* to the host, and said unto him, Take care of him; and whatsoever thou spendest more, when I come again, I will repay thee.

Which now of these three, thinkest thou, was neighbour unto him that fell among the thieves?
KJB   LUKE 10:30-36

When you love your neighbor as yourself, you are being a good neighbor and a good Samaritan.

An Old Salt

How many times have you heard someone say, "He is an old salt?" Or, "He is the salt of the earth?"

Ye are the salt of the earth: but if the salt have lost his savour, wherewith shall it be salted? it is thenceforth good for nothing, but to be cast out, and to be trodden under foot of men.
KJB   MATTHEW 5:13

We all know someone who we could call the salt of the earth. It's a person who we know will be there when we need him. It's someone who will not just help us, but a stranger in need as well. One that will guide us back to the right path.

Jacob's Ladder

And Jacob went out from Beersheba, and went toward Haran.

And he lighted upon a certain place, and tarried there all night, because the sun was set; and he took of the stones of that place, and put *them for* his pillows, and lay down in that place to sleep.

And he dreamed, and behold a ladder set up on the earth, and the top of it reached to heaven: and behold the angles of God ascending and descending on it.

And, behold, the LORD stood above it, and said, I *am* the LORD God of Abraham thy father, and the God of Isaac: the land whereon thou liest, to thee will I give it, and to thy seed;

And thy seed shall be as the dust of the earth, and thou shalt spread abroad to the west, and to the east, and to the north, and to the south: and in thee and in thy seed shall all the families of the earth be blessed.

And, behold, I *am* with thee, and will keep thee in all *places* whither thou goest, and will bring thee again into this land; for I will not leave thee, until I have done *that* which I have spoken to thee of.

And Jacob awaked out of his sleep, and he said, Surely the LORD is in this place; and I knew *it* not.

And he was afraid, and said, How dreadful *is* this place! this *is* none other but the house of GOD, and this *is* the gate of heaven.

And Jacob rose up early in the morning, and took the stone that he had put *for* his pillows, and set it up *for* a pillar, and poured oil upon the top of it.

And he called the name of that place Bethel: but the name of the city *was called* Luz at the first.

And Jacob vowed a vow, saying, If God will be with me, and will keep me in this way that I go, and will give me bread to eat, and raiment to put on,

So that I come again to my father's house in peace; then shall the LORD be my God:

And this stone, which I have set *for* a pillar, shall be God's house: and of all that thou shalt give me I will surely give the tenth unto thee.
KJB GENESIS 28-10-22

It is believed that the angels are God's messengers and that Jacob's prayers and God's answers were delivered through the angels.

The Lost Son And His Party

So when's the party going to be? Do you plan on killing the fattened calf?

This saying is from Jesus' parable "The Lost Son."

And the son said unto him, Father, I have sinned against heaven, and in thy sight, and am no more worthy to be called thy son.

But the father said to his servants, Bring forth the best robe, and put *it* on him; and put a ring on his hand, and shoes on *his* feet:

And bring hither the fatted calf, and kill *it*; and let us eat, and be merry:

For this my son was dead, and is alive again; he was lost, and is found. And they began to be merry.

KJB LUKE 15:21-24

My grandparents, Charles and Claira Nelson, and their ten children hosted a Christmas party in 1904. This took place on a farm in the Turtle Mountains of North Dakota. They did not kill the fatten calf. However, a calf was involved.

Grandpa knew of a bachelor living in a log cabin, who had a pump organ that wasn't being used. He managed to buy it for five dollars and a heifer calf.

My grandparent's Christmas present to their children was that organ. All 37 grandchildren can remember many gatherings around that organ singing hymns and Christmas carols.

What a fantastic gift in memories our grandparents gave to us.

The Cross I Have To Bear

"Oh yes, that's just one of the crosses I have to bear."

When you make the above statement, you are saying that something you have to do is similar to what Jesus went through when he died on the cross for our sins.

Please read JOHN 19:1-42.

After reading this chapter, I'm sure you will have a better understanding of what our Lord had to go through for our sins and to save us. Also look for the "fire insurance" policy that will keep you safe in his bosom.

Then came Jesus forth, wearing the crown of thorns, and the purple robe. And *Pilate* saith unto them, Behold the man!
KJB   JOHN 19:5

But they cried out, Away with *him*, away with *him*, crucify him. Pilate saith unto them, Shall I crucify your King? The chief priests answered, We have no king but Caesar.

Then delivered he him therefore unto them to be crucified. And they took Jesus, and led *him* away.

And he bearing his cross went forth into a place called *the place* of a skull, which is called in the Hebrew Golgotha:

Where they crucified him, and two other with him, on either side one, and Jesus in the midst.
KJB   JOHN 19:15-18

Please also read the prophet, ISAIAH 53.

Early To Bed, Early To Rise

Early to bed, early to rise, makes a person healthy, wealthy and wise.

It is vain for you to rise up early, to sit up late, to eat the bread of sorrows: *for* so he giveth his beloved sleep.

KJB   PSALMS 127:2

An Eye For An Eye

Some people express that they believe in an eye for an eye. If you ask them why, they will say because the Bible teaches it. When you ask them to show you where, they can't.

I ask, Is this what Jesus teaches? The answer is no.

Scripture says,

Ye have heard that it hath been said, An eye for an eye, and a tooth for a tooth:

But I say unto you, That ye resist not evil: but whosoever shall smite thee on thy right cheek, turn to him the other also.

And if any man will sue thee at the law, and take away thy coat, let him have *thy* cloak also.

And whosoever shall compel thee to go a mile, go with him twain.

KJB   MATTHEW 5:38-41

Jesus wants me to love my neighbor even when he has done something wrong to me. He wants me to love him and forgive him, just as Jesus has forgiven me.

The Apple Of My Eye

We have all heard the cliché, "He or she is the apple of my eye."

Our Lord felt this way about Moses.

He found him in a desert land, and in the waste howling wilderness; he led him about, he instructed him, he kept him as the apple of his eye.

KJB   DEUTERONOMY 32:10

It always amazes me how many phrases we use daily that are a part of God's word.

Two Are Better Than One

Two *are* better than one; because they have a good reward for their labour.

For if they fall, the one will lift up his fellow: But woe to him *that is* alone when he falleth; for *he hath* not another to help him up.
KJB   ECCLESIASTES 4:9-10

There are times when I'm working alone that I find I need help. I must call on a trusted friend to help me.

Tassels

Could it be that the tassel on the graduation cap was put there to remind you of what you have learned in school as in the Book of NUMBERS.

And the LORD spake unto Moses, saying,

Speak unto the children of Israel, and bid them that they make them fringes in the borders of their garments throughout their generations, and that they put upon the fringe of the borders a ribband of blue:

And it shall be unto you for a fringe, that ye may look upon it, and remember all the commandments of the LORD, and do them; and that ye seek not after your own heart and your own eyes, after which ye use to go a-whoring:

That ye may remember, and do all my commandments, and be holy unto your God.
KJB NUMBERS 15:37-40

A Little Bird Told Me

There are times when you ask someone, "Who told you that?" And they will answer, "Oh! A little bird told me."

Curse not the king, no not in thy thought; and curse not the rich in thy bedchamber: for a bird of the air shall carry the voice, and that which hath wings shall tell the matter.
KJB   ECCLESIASTES 10:20

A gossip is defined as a scandalmonger. Other definitions include: hearsay, rumor, scuttlebutt, a tattle or to disclose something often of questionable nature that is better kept to yourself.

Think about alternatives to talk about, such as books, vacations, theater, plays, sports and the Bible.

Rabble Rousers

We call people, who are never satisfied and those who complain about most things, "rabble rousers."

Did you know that this is how the Bible refers to the Israelites who complained to Moses about the manna?

They didn't like or grew tired of the manna that God provided for them in the desert. Instead, they wanted what they were used to in Egypt: fish, cucumbers, melons and leeks.

They forgot about the cruel treatment that Pharaoh put them under.

And the mixed multitude (rabble) that *was* among them fell a-lusting: and the children of Israel also wept again, and said, Who shall give us flesh to eat?

KJB   NUMBERS 11:4

Who Will Cast The First Stone?

Who is willing to cast the first stone?

The Pharisees brought a woman caught in adultery and asked Jesus if she should be stoned as commanded in Moses' law.

This they said, tempting him, that they might have to accuse him. But Jesus stooped down, and with *his* finger wrote on the ground, *as though he heard them not.*

So when they continued asking him, he lifted up himself, and said unto them, He that is without sin among you, let him first cast a stone at her.
KJB   JOHN 8:6-7

By The Sweat Of My Brow

I earned it by the sweat of my brow.

This came from the Book of GENESIS. God is explaining to Adam how he will have to earn his keep because of his sin.

In the sweat of thy face shalt thou eat bread, till thou return unto the ground; for out of it wast thou taken: for dust thou *art*, and unto dust shalt thou return.

KJB   GENESIS 3:19

The world changed when Adam and Eve chose to sin. We must earn our bread by the sweat of our brow. However, because we believe in Jesus Christ, we will have eternal life with him. We will live in paradise forever after this life.

Pillar Of The Community

He is one of the pillars of the community.

Paul, in the Book of GALTIANS, refers to James, Peter and John as pillars.

And when James, Cephas, and John, who seemed to be pillars, perceived the grace that was given unto me, they gave to me and Barnabas the right hands of fellowship; that we *should go* unto the heathen, and they unto the circumcision.

Only *they would* that we should remember the poor; the same which I also was forward to do.

KJB   GALATIANS 2:9-10

The Lord gives us leaders who sometimes stand out in our communities. They set examples for you and I, and most importantly, for our children.

This morning, as I sat near my window writing, the trash man came up the street. And when he emptied my neighbor's canister into his truck, a piece of paper fell on the street.

Rather than leave it, he picked it up. When he returned on the other side of the street. I went out and thanked him. He smiled and said, Thank you."

This man is also a pillar in my eyes because he took the time to care.

Leaning To The Right Or Left

We sometimes say, "Someone is leaning to the right." Or, we may say, "This person is leaning to the left."

Solomon refers to this in the Book of ECCLESIASTES.

A wise man's heart *is* at his right hand; but a fool's heart at his left.
KJB ECCLESIASTES 10:2

In today's 21st Century America, the interpretation is often political.

One that leans to the right is referred to as a right-winger or a conservative.

One that leans to the left is a left-winger or a liberal.

I Will Wash My Hands Of That

I'm going to wash my hands of this situation.

People say this when they get themselves into a situation they do not want to deal with, as Pilate did when he felt Jesus was unjustly accused.

Pilate saith unto them, What shall I do then with Jesus which is called Christ? *They* all say unto him, Let him be crucified.

And the governor said, Why, what evil hath he done? But they cried out the more, saying, Let him be crucified.

When Pilate saw that he could prevail nothing, but *that* rather a tumult was made, he took water, and washed *his* hands before the multitude, saying, I am innocent of the blood of this just person: see ye *to it*.

KJB   MATTHEW 27:22-24

A Black Sheep

He is the black sheep of our family. Or, we may say, "He is the lost sheep of our family."

I have gone astray like a lost sheep; seek thy servant; for I do not forget thy commandments.
KJB   PSALMS 119:176

What man of you, having an hundred sheep, if he lose one of them, doth not leave the ninety and nine in the wilderness, and go after that which is lost, until he find it?

And when he hath found *it*, he layeth *it* on his shoulders, rejoicing.

And when he cometh home, he calleth together *his* friends and neighbours, saying unto them, Rejoice with me; for I have found my sheep which was lost.

I say unto you, that likewise joy shall be in heaven over one sinner that repenteth, more than over ninety and nine just persons, which need no repentance.

KJB   LUKE 15:4-7

I am a grandfather and there are times when I take my grandchildren shopping. And if they wander off in a crowded store, how happy I am when I find them safe.

A Thorn In My Side

This situation has become a thorn in my side.

God is telling the Israelites to remove the Canaanites from the land or they will become a thorn in their side.

But if ye will not drive out the inhabitants of the land from before you; then it shall come to pass, that those which ye let remain of them *shall be* pricks in your eyes, and thorns in your sides, and shall vex you in the land wherein ye dwell.

KJB   NUMBERS 33:55

Wherefore I also said, I will not drive them out from before you; but they shall be *as thorns* in your sides, and their gods shall be a snare unto you.

KJB   JUDGES 2:3

Threescore And Ten Years

This is the average length of time God has given man to live.

The days of our years *are* threescore years and ten; and if by reason of strength *they be* fourscore years, yet *is* their strength labour and sorrow; for it is soon cut off, and we fly away.
KJB   PSALMS 90:10

We may have some seventy years in this life. It's really only a puff of smoke compared to the time we will be with our Father in eternity.

God gives us so much of his time. For us to give him ten minutes or more of our time each day isn't much, but it is a start. We can pray for our families, ministers, missionaries, and teachers. We must be specific when praying. Name the person and ask God to bless marriages, friendships, their Christian walk or whatever their need may be.

Whoever Strikes You On Your Cheek

If someone strikes us on the cheek, are we to turn so he can also strike us on the other?

Bless them that curse you, and pray for them which despitefully use you.

And unto him that smiteth thee on the *one* cheek offer also the other; and him that taketh away the cloak forbid not *to take thy* coat also.
KJB   LUKE 6:28-29

Our nature is to strike back when someone hurts us. But if over and over again I show kindness to that person, he or she may begin to see the wrong they did and to rectify their action.

A Lot Of Gall

When someone says, "That man or woman has a lot of gall," it means there's a bitter taste towards the offender's action.

This word comes from when Jesus was crucified on the cross.

And when they were come unto a place called Golgotha, that is to say, a place of a skull,

They gave him vinegar to drink mingled with gall: and when he had tasted *thereof*, he would not drink.

KJB   MATTHEW 27:33-34

Am I My Brother's Keeper?

Cain was asked by God, Where is your brother Abel?

And Cain talked with Abel his brother: and it came to pass, when they were in the field, that Cain rose up against Abel his brother, and slew him.

And the LORD said unto Cain, Where *is* Abel, thy brother? And he said, I know not: *Am* I my brother's keeper?
KJB   GENESIS 4:8-9

Christ teaches us to always help our neighbor when he is in need.

What You Sow, You Will Also Reap

How many times has someone said to you, "Just remember, what you sow, you will also reap?"

Even as I have seen, they that plow iniquity, and sow wickedness, reap the same.
KJB   JOB 4:8

Be not deceived; God is not mocked: for whatsoever a man soweth, that shall he also reap.
KJB   GALATIANS 6:7

The Handwriting On The Wall

I can see the handwriting on the wall.

When King Nebuchadnizzar, King of Babylon, came to Jerusalem and besieged it, he carried back to Babylon all the gold and silver vessels and brought them into the treasury of his God.

Years later his son Belshazzer had the vessels brought out so he and one thousand of his nobles, their wives and concubines could drink out of them.

The Bible says in DANIEL:

They drank wine, and praised the gods of gold, and of silver, of brass, of iron, of wood, and of stone.

In the same hour came forth fingers of a man's hand, and wrote over against the candlestick upon the plaster of the wall of the king's palace: and the king saw the part of the hand that wrote.

KJB   DANIEL 5:4-5

Train Up A Child

Train up a child in the way he should go: and when he is old, he will not depart from it.
KJB   PROVERBS 22:6

We think of old as when our hair turns to gray or when we are in the senior years of our lives.

The Hebrew meaning in this proverb is when the young man grows hair on his chin or, in today's America, when a girl grows hair on her legs.

Note: In training a child, accept your child's strong and good points.

Never correct in anger, always attack the problem not the person.

Noah's Rainbow

Did you know that God made the rainbow for Noah and for us to signify that the rains were over and that the planet earth would never again see a world flood?

I do set my bow in the cloud, and it shall be for a token of a covenant between me and the earth,

And it shall come to pass, when I bring a cloud over the earth, that the bow shall be seen in the cloud:

And I will remember my covenant, which *is* between me and you and every living creature of all flesh; and the waters shall no more become a flood to destroy all flesh.

And the bow shall be in the cloud; and I will look upon it, that I may remember the everlasting covenant between God and every living creature of all flesh that *is* upon the earth.

And God said unto Noah, This *is* the token of the covenant, which I have established between me and all flesh that *is* upon the earth.
KJB   GENESIS 9:13-17

He Who Harbors Anger

We all harbor anger at times towards someone who we feel has wronged us.

We need to work through this anger. It will affect our work, free time and our lives.

Recompense to no man evil for evil. Provide things honest in the sight of all men.

If it be possible, as much as lieth in you, live peaceably with all men.

Dearly beloved, avenge not yourselves, but *rather* give place unto wrath: for it is written, Vengeance *is* mine; I will repay, saith the Lord.

Therefore if thine enemy hunger, feed him; if he thirst, give him drink: for in so doing thou shalt heap coals of fire on his head.

Be not overcome of evil, but overcome evil with good.

KJB   ROMANS 12:17-21

I have learned to pray for those who may have wronged me and also for myself for I may have caused their reaction.

We must continue praying each day until our anger has been removed. This may take a long time, but God is faithful. He will remove it.

Temptation

We all have experienced temptation. The devil is always at our door tempting us to sin.

Temptation itself is not sin, but willfully placing oneself in the way of temptation eventually may result in sinful acts.

When this happens we can send up a prayer to our Lord for help.

"Lord, help me to overcome this temptation."

There hath no temptation taken you but such as is common to man: but God *is* faithful, who will not suffer you to be tempted above that ye are able; but will with the temptation also make a way to escape, that ye may be able to bear *it*.
KJB   1 CORINTHIANS 10:13

Knowing Right From Wrong

Man makes laws and then tries to follow them. Each person has his own intuition as to what is right and what is wrong.

God has made laws for birds. It's called "instinct."

Papa Duck, Mama Duck and Little Duck were sitting on this lake up in the north country and the snow started to come down.

Papa Duck looked all around and then he put his head under his wing. When he brought it out, he said, "Mama Duck, Little Duck, my instinct tells me it is time to fly south. What about you Mama Duck?"

So Mama Duck put her head under her wing and after a bit she pulled it out and said, "Papa Duck, you're right. My instinct tells me it's time to fly south also. What about you Little Duck? We've taught you to swim, forage for food and fly. Now why don't you try."

So Little Duck put his head under his wing and when he pulled it out, he said, "Papa Duck, Mama Duck, my end stinks. But it doesn't tell me which way to fly."

People can follow their instincts, but remember we are not birds. We can seek out our answers from trusted friends, the Bible and prayer.

The Lord's Prayer

Jesus tells us in the Book of MATTHEW, how we should pray.

Our Father which art in heaven, Hallowed be thy name.

Thy kingdom come. Thy will be done in earth, as *it is* in heaven.

Give us this day our daily bread.

And forgive us our debts, as we forgive our debtors.

And lead us not into temptation, but deliver us from evil: For thine is the kingdom, and the power, and the glory, for ever. Amen.

KJB   MATTHEW 6:9-13

Forgiven

How do we know when we are forgiven? When I was fourteen my minister, Pastor C.A. Gisselquist, gave me a book by A.W. Knock, titled "The Way of Life."

The chapter on "Forgiven" gave me the peace I was looking for.

Am I forgiven? How can I know?

Perhaps you have not known the great joy of being assured that you are forgiven. Perhaps you hoped for or you longed to be assured. At one time you may have had the assurance of forgiveness but soon that joyous feeling was gone.

Do you recall when as a child you were naughty? Did you try to cover up your sin to conceal it from mother? No matter how hard you tried to cover it up and to forget it, you found no peace until you confessed to mother. How good it felt to unburden your heart, and above all, to hear her say, "Yes, I forgive you."

The word of God says,

I, *even* I, *am* he that blotteth out thy transgressions for mine own sake, and will not remember thy sins.
KJB   ISAIAH 43:25

When you have confessed and claimed the blood of Christ as cleansing for your sin, they are forgiven. And God forgets them. Why shouldn't you? Satan does not want you to forget them, but to continue to be troubled over them. Whom shall you believe, God or Satan?

God has also said,

As far as the east is from the west, *so* far hath he removed our transgressions from us.
KJB   PSALMS 103:12

How far is the east from the west? You cannot measure it. Similarly, your sins are far removed from you when forgiven.

Suppose a child asked Mother for forgiveness and heard her say, "I forgive you." What if that child returned in an hour and says, "Mother, I'm still feeling sorry for my sin. Won't you forgive me?"

If after another hour, during the next day and the next week, the child did the same, how would Mother like it?

Every time the child comes again to ask for forgiveness it calls Mother a liar. Why should you by your unbelief call God a liar? He has said, "If we confess our sins, he is faithful." Let us go by his word and not by our feelings. And let us not allow Satan to cause us to doubt God's word.

But if you cannot believe your sins are forgiven, so as to forget them, you will need to examine your own heart. Perhaps you have wronged someone so that you will need to ask forgiveness. Or you may need to make restitution. Ask the Lord to show you if there is anything in your life that needs to be set aright. Then, wait on him. And if he continues to point out your sin asking you to make amends, do as he directs. Your heart will be set at ease and you will find peace. Then rest in his promise,

"I will not remember thy sins."

A Colony Of Water Bugs And The Five Spiritual Laws

A colony of small water bugs living in a pond noticed that every once in a while one of their fellow bugs would climb up a lily stem and never be seen again. They agreed that if this should ever happen to one of them, they would return to tell the others about their journey.

Sure enough, the day came when one of the bugs found he was going up the stalk and crawling onto the lily pad. At the top he fell asleep in the warm sunshine and when he woke up, he stretched himself only to hear a crackling sound as his old coat fell off.

He sensed that somehow he was larger, cleaner and had more freedom than ever before. Spreading his wings, he flew into the air as a beautiful, green dragonfly. Suddenly, he remembered his promise then realized why none of the others had ever returned.

He couldn't go back and tell his friends what to expect because he was no longer a part of their world. Besides one day they would experience the wonderful freedom he now enjoyed.

We naturally shrink from the mysterious thought of dying, but we need to have faith in Christ that he will be there to help us.

You have many who love you. Ask a family member or friend to kneel down with you then say the following words.

(1) I realize that sin means death.
    ROMANS 6:23 (TLB)
    This tells us that the wages of sin is death, but the free gift of God is eternal life through Jesus Christ our Lord.

(2) I acknowledge my sinful state and need of God.
    ROMANS 3:23 (TLB)
    All have sinned. All fall short of God's glorious ideal.

(3) I recognize God's love for me.
    JOHN 3:16 (TLB)
    For God loved the world so much that he gave his only son so that anyone who believes in him shall not perish, but have eternal life.

(4) I receive you Jesus Christ and your forgiveness. And I know that you are the only way to God.
JOHN 1:12 (TLB)
But all who received him he gave the right to become children of God. All they needed to do was to trust him to save them.
ACTS 4:12 (TLB)
There is salvation in no one else! Under all heaven, there is no other name for men to call upon to save them.

(5) I commit myself totally to God's plan for my life.
ROMANS 10:9-13 (TLB)

For if you tell others with your own mouth that Jesus Christ is your Lord and believe in your own heart that God will raise you from the dead, you will be saved. For it is by believing in his heart that a man becomes right with God; and with his mouth he tells others of his faith, confirming his salvation. For the scripture tells us that no one who believes in Christ will ever be disappointed. Jews and Gentiles are the same in this respect. They all have the same Lord who generously gives his riches to all those who ask him. Anyone who calls upon the name of the Lord will be saved.

Once you have completed these steps, whatever you have said or done in the past is forgiven. Christ says, "I will forgive you as far as the east is from the west and I will not remember your sins."

Now that you have come to Christ, go to a happy, healthy, well-balanced Bible-believing church.

Get baptized and care for yourself by making sure you're taught the same principles that Jesus taught.

About The Author

Morey Lokken accepted Jesus Christ as his Lord and Savior when he was fourteen. While living in Mission Viejo, Calif., a friend asked him to join him in a Bible study fellowship. The year was 1974 and Morey attended that study group for eight years. He has been back for other studies with the group

He also participated in Bruce Wilkinson's study, "Read Through the Bible in One Year," for three years.

In reading the Bible, Morey found several clichés and phrases commonly used today.

Morey can be contacted at moreymal@hotmail.com